© Noëlle Writes, 2025

Graphic: Noëlle Writes

Publishing: BoD · Books on Demand GmbH
Überseering 33
22297 Hamburg
bod@bod.de
ISBN: 978-3-8192-9920-9

Printing: Libri Plureos GmbH,
Friedensallee 273,
22763 Hamburg

Hello Mums. Hello Dads. Hello Parents.

It's great that this book has found its way to you. It is intended to be an inspiration for mums and dads – and parents. The book contains questions to help mums and dads to reflect more deeply on becoming and being a mum/dad and to strengthen yourselves as individuals, but also as a couple.

My wish with this book is that

- you gain an even deeper awareness of becoming and being a mum/dad
- you gain valuable insights into becoming and being a mum/dad
- connecting conversations between parents, but also between different mums and dads, arise
- an open and honest exchange is created
- individual and mutual learning takes place
- mutual understanding between mums and dads is strengthened
- you have lots of fun reflecting and exchanging your experiences as mum/dad

The idea for this book came about when my daughter was around five months old. I realised how numerous, complex and profound the changes are that go hand in hand with becoming and being a parent. I realised:

When two people suddenly become three (at least with the first child), life changes fundamentally – on many levels. The familiar togetherness gives way to a new form of togetherness: the trinity. The well-rehearsed duo becomes a team with an extended range of responsibilities – including parenthood.

This new phase of life brings with it many changes – not only in everyday life, but also in the relationship. The roles shift. You experience yourself and your partner in a new way. Decisions must be made together more often and compromises are suddenly on the agenda. Shared responsibility can strengthen the bond between partners – but it can also put a strain on it. Feelings of closeness and deep

connection can arise as well as moments of excessive demands or even loneliness.

Being a parent brings a whole range of emotions into play – often more intense than you would have expected. The feelings range from love, gratitude and joy to worry, exhaustion and uncertainty to inner emptiness – and sometimes all in a single day. Especially in the early days, when everything is new (and the hormones are doing their bit), there can be a veritable flood of emotions. Some emotions are familiar, while others are so new that we first must learn to categorise and understand them.

Everyday life also changes: Daily routines, leisure time, nights – everything is structured differently. Your own needs and interests take a back seat for the time being, while the child takes centre stage. This can bring with it a feeling of being controlled by others, which many parents first must come to terms with.

It is not uncommon for a child to also bring about changes in their career and financial situation. Whether it's an adjustment to working hours, a redistribution of tasks or a change to the previous standard of living – many things must be reconsidered and reorganised.

The changes described here are certainly only a small part of what being a parent entails. How far-reaching these changes are depending very much on the individual life situation – and of course also on how each mum and dad ticks.

Becoming and being a parent is deeply personal. Some topics are fraught with uncertainty or even shame. Not everyone finds it easy to access their own mum or dad hood. It can be difficult to talk about what you have experienced. And yet this is precisely where a great opportunity lies: to face yourself honestly, to exchange ideas, to consciously come to terms with this new role. All of this can have a

liberating effect – in your head, in your heart, in your behaviour and in your everyday life.

I sincerely wish you as a mum/dad and you as parents, lots of joy with the following questions. May you gain wonderful, inspiring, instructive and transformative insights about yourselves as individuals, but also about yourselves as parents.

Reflection questions for you as a mum/dad

These questions relate to your own view of becoming and being a mum/dad. You can answer them on your own and take notes if you wish. It can also be interesting and valuable to share your thoughts with the other parent or to talk to other mums and dads about their experiences.

What does becoming
and being a mum/dad
mean to you in ONE
WORD?

What do you find beautiful and enriching about being a mum/dad?

What do you find
challenging and
exhausting about being
a mum/dad?

What has surprised you
the most about
becoming and being a
mum/dad?

How do you perceive
yourself
as a mum/dad?

When do you feel secure
as a mum/dad

-

and when do you feel
insecure?

Which of your skills help you particularly in everyday life with your child?

What are you particularly proud of in your role as a mum/dad?

What helped you to find your way into the mum/dad role?

**What do you need to feel
seen and understood as
a mum/dad?**

How do you deal with
the feeling of not being
able to do everything
justice?

What gives you strength
when you are exhausted
from being a mum/dad?

Which situations in
being a mum/dad
push you to your
emotional limits

-

and how do you deal
with them?

How do you look after your own needs in everyday family life?

**Which parts of your own
mum/dad
have you consciously or
unconsciously adopted?**

What do you wish you
had known before you
became a mum/dad?

Which ideas about being
a mum/dad have turned
out to be correct?

Which ideas about being
a mum/dad have turned
out to be wrong?

How have you changed since you became a mum/dad?

How has your life
changed since you
became a mum/dad?

How has your emotional
state changed since you
became a mum/dad?

How have your thoughts
changed since you
became a mum/dad?

How has your behaviour
changed since you
became a mum/dad?

How has your attitude to
life changed since you
became a mum/dad?

How has your view of
the world changed since
you became a
mum/dad?

How has your
relationship changed
since you became a
mum/dad?

How has your
relationship with your
own parents changed
since you became a
mum/dad?

How have your
relationships with your
friends changed since
you became a
mum/dad?

How has your attitude
towards employment
changed since you
became a mum/dad?

What would you do differently today than when you first became and were a mum/dad – and why?

What has becoming and
being a mum/dad taught
you about yourself?

In which moments do
you feel gratitude for
becoming and being a
mum/dad?

What would you say to
your younger self today

-

shortly before the birth
of your child?

Assuming your child is
expecting a child of
his/her own one day:
What would you give
him/her along the way?

Assuming your friend is
expecting a child one
day, what would you give
him/her along the way?

What would you like to
tell your child about
becoming and being a
mum/dad when they are
older?

How would you like to
be remembered as a
mum/dad?

Reflection questions for you as parents

The following questions concern you as parents and your mutual view of becoming and being a mum/dad. You can answer them together as parents. You can either prepare yourselves individually or work on the questions directly together.

How do you perceive
each other in your role
as parents?

What changes have you
noticed in the other
since becoming a
mum/dad?

What surprised you
about the other in terms
of the role as mum/dad?

Are there any implicit
expectations
you have of each other
as mum/dad?

What do you appreciate
about the other in
relation to being a
mum/dad?

What do you find challenging about being a mum/dad?

How can you support
each other in terms of
being a mum/dad

-

where is there potential
for optimisation?

What are your current needs and how are they currently satisfied?

What do you need to feel confident and competent in your role as a parent?

How much space do you give each other for personal interests and individual development?

What are your greatest
joys in relation to being
a parent?

What are your biggest
fears or worries in
relation to being a
parent?

How do you deal with
stress or exhaustion
when being a parent?

What have you learnt from your child about yourselves?

In which moments do
you feel really
connected as parents

-

and when do you feel
more separated?

How does being a parent
affect your relationship
as a couple

-

positive and negative?

How important is time
together as a couple
besides being parents?

What rituals or habits
strengthen you as a
parent team?

How can you better
resolve conflicts about
being parents together?

Are there topics in being
a parent that you have
not talked enough about
so far?

What have you always
wanted to say to
yourselves about being
parents?

What have you always
wanted to thank each
other for in terms of
being parents?

Reflection on the reflections

- How did you feel when reflecting on the questions?

- What was easy for you to reflect on and what was more difficult?

- What insights did you gain about yourself as a mum/dad, about the other parent and about you as a couple?

- How could you integrate regular reflection on being a mum/dad and being parents into your everyday life?